Bitcoin Beginne
How You Can Profit from
Trading and Investing in
Bitcoin

By Stephen Satoshi

Table of Contents

are done without written consent and can in no way be considered an endorsement from the trademark holder.

Financial Disclaimer:

I am not a financial advisor, this is not financial advice. This is not an investment guide nor investment advice. I am not recommending you buy any of the coins listed here. Any form of investment or trading is liable to lose you money.

There is no single "best" investment to be made, in cryptocurrencies or otherwise. Anyone telling you so is deceiving you.

There is no "surefire coin" - one again, anyone telling you so is deceiving you.

With many coins, especially the smaller ones, the market is liable to the spread of misinformation.

Never invest more than you are willing to lose. Cryptocurrency is not a get rich quick scheme.

Introduction

This is normally the part with the drier than the Sahara Desert explanation of "you are going to learn blah blah..." that sends you straight to sleep.

Instead, I thought I'd do something a bit different and give you a quick overview of my own experience with Bitcoin.

I first heard of Bitcoin in 2011, during the first very first bubble, when I read a news report about this "internet money" thing that was worth $30 a piece. Did I invest then? I wish - I wasn't nearly informed enough. I honestly didn't understand how the technology worked or if Bitcoin was worth anything at all. After all, if a currency isn't backed by a government, how *can* it be worth anything? Oh to be that naive once again.

By the time I finally understood Bitcoin enough to be confident in buying some, the price had risen a hell of a lot more. But, now I believe in it as more than just a commodity to be traded or invested in. I believe in the technology at its core, and the potentially game changing ramifications for society at large. In that lies the true value of Bitcoin.

I wish I had a resource like this when I started out, something that explained the core concepts of Bitcoin and blockchain technology without reading like an astrophysics phD thesis. That's precisely why I wrote this book.

Happy reading, and I hope you not only make a lot of money with Bitcoin - I hope it has a truly profound and positive effect on your life.

Thanks,

Stephen

Bitcoin - A Brief History

Bitcoin is the first cryptocurrency that has lasted for more than 7 years and received any sort of mass adoption, but it took some time to get to this point. Before Bitcoin, there were a number of cryptocurrencies that reached some level of popularity. It all started back in 1980 when cryptographer David Chaum first developed the idea of a currency backed by a proof-of-work computer algorithm as opposed to a central bank. Chaum later went on to found DigiCash which had a briefly successful yet ultimately failed run at becoming the world's first mass adopted cryptocurrency. US based e-gold was possibly the most notable of the Pre-Bitcoin cryptocurrencies, although technologically it was significantly different from Bitcoin due to a centralized owner and non-fixed supply.

In August 2008, Neal Kin, Vladimir Oksman and Charles Bry filed a patent application for an encryption technology. The domain name Bitcoin.org was also registered in the same month using anonymousspeech.com which allowed for anonymous domain name registrations.

The big day came on October 31st 2008, Satoshi Nakamoto (a pseudonym with the true identity still unconfirmed) published a white paper named "Bitcoin: A Peer-to-Peer Electronic Cash System". The paper outlined various uses for the coin in addition to providing information about blockchain technology and how the coin would be mined using computer algorithms. The original white paper used Bitcoin as an example of a deflationary currency and one that governments or other central lenders could not artificially increase the money supply of, therefore devaluing a certain currency. The whitepaper also outlined issues with banks as trusted lenders, and how the blockchain's irreversible transaction design could reduce risk of fraud for merchants.

From January 2009 onwards, activists began mining the coin and the first Bitcoin blocks were created. Nakamoto and other cryptography enthusiasts began exchanging the coin for services with one another and in October 2009, the first official exchange rate was established for the coin of US$1 = 1,309.03 BTC. The original exchange rate was based on how much electricity it would cost to mine 1 Bitcoin.

The first real world transaction took place in May 2010 when enthusiast Laszlo Hanyecz bought two pizzas in Jacksonville, Florida for 10,000 BTC. Today 10,000BTC is worth over $40 million. A few months later in August, the first major Bitcoin hacking incident occured, the hacker exploited a vulnerability in the Bitcoin verification system and generated 184 billion Bitcoins. This led to the first major dip in the value of Bitcoin as a currency. This then led to government investigations of potential money laundering using Bitcoin. The early scares didn't last long though and In November 2010, Bitcoin reached a market capitalization of $1 million for the first time.

In January 2011, Bitcoin received a reasonable amount of mainstream coverage for the first time. Silk Road, an underground dark net website dealing in illicit goods such as illegal drugs and stolen credit cards was launched on the back of sending and receiving payments in Bitcoin. At its peak, it was estimated that up to 50% of Bitcoin transactions were ones that occured on Silk Road. The perceived anonymity of Bitcoin made it a favorite among Silk Road users. In February, Bitcoin reaches a market price of $1 for the first time and by July the coin had jumped to a value of $31.

2012 was somewhat of an uneventful year, although real world adoption continued with hosting platform Wordpress accepting the coin in November of that year. By March 2013, the market capitalization had reached $1 billion and Bitcoin exchange Coinbase reported over $1 million of Bitcoin transactions in a single month. In June, the DEA reported 11.02 Bitcoins as an asset during a drug seizure, the first time a government agency recognized Bitcoin as having inherent value. Drugs continued to make headlines as Silk Road owner Ross William Albricht was arrested in October, the FBI seized 26,000 Bitcoins from Silk Road servers during the arrest. Brighter news came the next month when the world's first Bitcoin ATM opened in Vancouver and China arrived on the scene when Chinese market activity overtook the US for the first time. By November of 2013, the price of 1 Bitcoin reached $1,000 for the first time.

December of 2013 came with China's central bank ruling that Bitcoin was not a currency and barred financial institution from accepting Bitcoins as a form of payment. In February 2014, Japanese based exchange Mt. Gox suspended Bitcoin withdrawals, citing technical issues. Within just a few weeks, the exchange had filed for bankruptcy amid claims of poor management and lack of security protocols. Roughly $740 million worth of Bitcoin, or 7% of the overall amount in circulation was lost in the incident. This issue led to the value of Bitcoin dropping 36% over the course of the month.

In June, TeraExchange LLC received approval from the U.S.Commodity Futures Trading Commission. This marked the first time that a U.S. agency approved a Bitcoin exchange. Computer manufacturer Dell began accepting Bitcoin as a means of payment at this time, the largest company to do so up to that point. AirBaltic also became the world's first airline to accept Bitcoin payments. In December, tech giant Microsoft began accepting payments in Bitcoin.

Coinbase, now one of the largest cryptocurrency exchange platforms received $75 million in a funding round, with the New York Stock Exchange being a minor investor. Further real world scaling continued and by August 2015, over 160,000 companies were accepting Bitcoin as a means of payment. December brought news of the potential identity of the notorious Satoshi Nakamoto figure. Wired magazine claimed the Australian Craig Wright was indeed Nakamoto. This led to a series of events that eventually resulted in a confirmation that Wright was indeed NOT Nakamoto.

July 2016 marked the second "halving day" in Bitcoin's history, where the reward for mining 1 block was halved to 12.5 Bitcoins per block. This was part of Bitcoin's original design to gradually decrease the supply of new coins available. The next halving is due to occur in 2020, with the total supply available to the market around the year 2140.

At the time of writing, Bitcoin trades for around $4,000 per coin on exchanges.

Basics of Blockchain Technology

While we could spend an entire book on blockchain and the technology behind it alone, it is important to understand the fundamentals if you're planning to invest in Bitcoin, or any other cryptocurrency.

Blockchain is a decentralized ledger, meaning it is a record that is publicly accessible and can be verified by anyone. This is important for any non-tangible good as the unlike tangible goods like socks or candy, we need a record of a transaction happening in case something goes wrong. For example, we need proof that Steve paid John for the pair of socks that John sold him. The blockchain will have a record of a transaction from Steve's account to John's account, and no one else's.

Previously, we would have the use a third party, like a bank, to verify the transaction did indeed take place. The bank would then take their % of the total transaction. As the bank information is not publicly accessible, we would also have to trust that the bank did their job. By using blockchain technology, we have a 100% infallible record of the transaction taking place, and anyone can see this. There's also no need to pay a large additional fee to a middleman. The only fee involved is the cost of running the blockchain itself.

If we only use blockchain for financial purposes, this is extremely useful in countries that do not have a trustworthy banking sector. Each transaction is recorded as a block, with a date and timestamp. These blocks cannot be altered without everyone seeing. The problem this solves is known as the "double-spending problem", where digital assets (like cryptocurrency) have the potential to be spent more than once. What the blockchain allows us to do is see that Steve has already used his money to pay John, so he can't then use that same money to try and pay Sally. The blockchain creates trust among all parties, and trust is paramount when dealing with monetary transactions.

Blockchain's uses are not strictly financial. We can also use the technology to store other information that we would need in a publicly available, transparent form. This ranges from anything like voting records in an election, to a self-executing contract between two parties that fulfills when both parties have completed their obligations. Blockchain eliminates the need for a middleman, or independent auditor in these situation, as the technology itself acts both as an auditor, and as an independent. In theory, the technology has the power to replace accountants, lawyers and much of the financial services industry. Before we get ahead of ourselves though, much of the non-financial uses of blockchain technology are still strictly, in theory.

How does Bitcoin Work?

Bitcoin functions as a digital currency, by following the same three rules that traditional, or fiat currencies follow.

1. They need to be difficult to produce (cash) or find (gold or other precious metals)

2. They need have a limited supply

3. They need to be recognized by other humans as having value

When we examine Bitcoin, it ticks the boxes of all three of these characteristics:

1. Bitcoin uses complex computer algorithms in its production which take a lot of computational power and proof-of-work, so it cannot be replicated easily or at a discount

2. There are a finite supply of Bitcoins - 21 Million to be exact. As of 2015, roughly 2/3 of this number had been mined

3. There are hundreds of Bitcoin exchanges and Bitcoin is accepted as payment everywhere from Subway to OKCupid

Bitcoin miners have incentive to mine as they receive Bitcoin as a reward for their computer's endeavors. Bitcoin was designed to be a deflationary currency, so unlike fiat currencies, the supply of money is fixed. This, combined with the decentralization principle ensure that no single person or government can simply create additional coins once the supply is mined. Once all the coins are mined, the value of the currency will in theory, continue to rise.

Bitcoin transactions are recorded on a digital ledger (or record) known as the blockchain. The core concept that upholds Bitcoin's usefulness is decentralization. With decentralization, the blockchain is not owned by one single person or entity. In fact, everyone has access to it. Therefore transactions are publicly broadcasted across the network, which ensures that both parties have upheld their end of the agreement. The code is open source (like Linux or Android Operating Systems) so anyone can view it, this ensures transparency among all parties.

Decentralization allows the blockchain to be secured by multiple points of entry and backed up by multiple points of failure. This is turn prevents incidents like hacking or theft. For example, if someone offers you 1 Bitcoin, you can check the blockchain records to make sure that Bitcoin is valid and hasn't already been spent. This system means we do not need third parties to validate the transactions. The only transactions costs come from the electricity or mining power needed to run the blockchain itself.

This has tremendous real world application, from allowing cheaper international payments (since Bitcoin has no nationality) to lowering the overall price of certain goods.

Bitcoin as a Store of Wealth

Bitcoin's status as a deflationary currency makes it incredibly useful in times where fiat currency is undergoing gross levels of inflation. Like gold has been traditionally used in times of economic hardship, Bitcoin has the potential to do the same. To be used as a store of value or wealth, Bitcoin has a fulfill a few criteria.

1. It has to not be perishable
2. It has to not depreciate over time

The second criteria is somewhat debatable, as critics argue that Bitcoin could depreciate due to better technology surpassing it. However, Bitcoin has now reached a certain market point where the idea itself has an intrinsic value, like say email or Facebook. Email isn't particularly useful if you're the only one with an address to send mail to, but the more people use the technology, the easier, and more valuable it is.

Venezuela is currently undergoing the worst cash crisis of the decade. Inflation has reached a level where people's money is nigh-on worthless against the US dollar, and much of the country cannot afford basic necessities. That is, except for those who hold Bitcoins, whose value against the US dollar continues to increase.

China is doing the same thing, albeit for different reasons. Traditional investments in Chinese assets have returned less than previous years due to the government's devaluation of the Yuan. Converting money to gold and silver is heavily regulated and often incurs large transaction costs. Bitcoin does not suffer from any of these issues, and often is the only alternative for those who are looking to secure their wealth in both the short and long term.

Gold has long been the traditional backup plan, or "hedge" against uncertain financial markets. In times of war, or financial crisis, gold prices tend to rise when financial markets are falling. However, in recent times this has not been the case. At the time of writing, gold's 12 month performance is stagnant, whereas Bitcoin has risen by nearly 1000%. Growing tensions in North Korea are just one factor that has spurned Bitcoin's growth in times of uncertainty. Tensions in the region have led to increased buys from the Chinese, Japanese and South Korean markets.

8 Common Bitcoin Myths Debunked

Like all technological innovations, there are a number of points that uninformed players do not understand. As such, misinformation spreads which causes fear, uncertainty and doubt - which only hurts the technology going forward.

1. Bitcoin is illegal

Let's deal with the big one off the bat shall we? Just because a currency is not backed by a government, does not make it illegal. For you, the user, by operating as a virtual currency, Bitcoin is legal, so long as you are using it for legal means.

2. Miners or developers can change the amount of Bitcoins available to benefit themselves

The way the Bitcoin algorithm works ensures there are no shortcuts in obtaining one. If a counterfeit Bitcoin does not satisfy all the conditions required, any transactions made using it will be rejected. This is similar to how banks reject counterfeit bank notes.

3. Bitcoin isn't worth anything because it isn't
    backed by a central government

With all currencies, they are only worth what
someone is willing to exchange for them. In the same
way that gold or US dollars have no inherent value,
Bitcoin is just a means of exchange.

4. Bitcoin's main use is for criminals and the
    government will shut it down

Yes, at one time a significant % of Bitcoin usage was
used for illegal activity. Much of this activity was
facilitated on the underground black market website
Silk Road. However, this is no longer the case. Bitcoin
is now accepted by over 160,000 merchants
worldwide and adoption continues to grow. The
technological uses like minimized transactions fees
have far more use for large financial institutions than
they do for some basement dwelling 20 year trying to
buy LSD from a guy in another country. It's worth
noting that fiat currencies are also used for criminal
activity.

This one also relies on the myth that Bitcoin is completely anonymous. Yes, there are no named Bitcoin accounts, but each Bitcoin address is unique and every transaction is recorded on a public ledger (the blockchain). Therefore with a little legwork, it is possible to determine who is behind a Bitcoin transaction.

As far as a potential government shutdown does, that's a little trickier. Governments do have the power to make life difficult for citizens dealing strictly in Bitcoin, but this difficulty only goes as far as taxation on Bitcoin.

5.   21 Million Bitcoins is too small of a total number for effective daily use

Where this one falls short is that it fails to compute that Bitcoin is divisible to eight decimal places. 0.00000001 BTC is actually the smallest unit available, this is also known as 1 Satoshi. There are really 2,099,999,997,690,000 (just over 2 quadrillion) maximum possible units or Satoshi in the Bitcoin system. When 1 Bitcoin becomes too large for day-to-day transactions, we will simply move on to smaller units for convenience, similar to how we use pennies now for small transactions.

6.   Hackers can simply steal all the Bitcoins

It's important to differentiate between exchanges or websites being hacked, and the blockchain itself being hacked. Exchange hacks exploit security weaknesses of private companies, whereas the blockchain is not centralized so there is no single weakness for hackers to exploit. The same argument can be applied to the US dollar, just because a store is robbed does not mean the US dollar as a currency has been stolen from the source. That said, you should take appropriate security precautions when storing your Bitcoin such as creating a safe, offline wallet.

7. Bitcoin is a pyramid scheme/Ponzi scheme

My personal favorite. Pyramid schemes are a zero sum game. The founders and early adopters profit from the money put into the scheme by late adopters. With Bitcoin everyone can profit, no matter when they first made their initial investment. The other illusion here is that there is one central founder of Bitcoin. Bitcoin is decentralized and there is no "CEO" or person at the top of the pyramid.

8. Bitcoin is dead/There is no point investing in Bitcoin now

I have witnessed at least 20 "Bitcoin deaths" in the past 5 years alone. From hacking incidents to Silk Road Founder Ross William Albricht's arrest, detractors have used these as fuel for Bitcoin's obtituary. The numbers don't lie though, and Bitcoin is in a stronger position than ever both in terms of market capitalization and real world adoption.

As early as 2012, you can find commentators saying it was "too late" to invest in Bitcoin. Yet, real world adoption continues to grow, and the price keeps on rising. Is that to say there won't be issues in the future? I'm sure there will be. However, if Bitcoin transactions keep increasing, the currency shows no signs of slowing down any time soon.

Latest Bitcoin Innovations: SegWit, Lightning Network

The number one technical issue Bitcoin faces in its lifetime is the issue of scalability. Or in real world terms, Bitcoin's ability to handle a growing number of transactions. Currently, each Block on the Bitcoin network is 1MB, representing 10 minutes per transaction, which increases during periods of heavy use. This is beneficial for banks and large financial institutions as 10 minutes is a far quicker processing time than that of say SWIFT or other payment networks. However, in terms of smaller businesses, like say a coffee shop, 10 minutes is an incredibly long and non-practical payment time.

For years, there has been a constant disagreement about the best way to upgrade Bitcoin's block sizes. The longer these arguments continue, the slower any proposed solutions are developed. There are two main camps, those who favor a hard fork, which loosens up the rules of the protocol and those who favor a soft fork, which tightens the rules of the current protocol.

Without going into advanced technical details, users who favor a soft fork are currently proposing a solution known as Segregated Witness or SegWit. The crux of SegWit is that the signature (or *witness)* of a transaction can be kept on a separate block from the transaction itself, this frees up block space for additional transactions. The witness data is encrypted and cannot be modified, so there is no ability to change the information of the payment sender. This has great real world usage in terms of lowering the ability to hack a transaction.

As with any potential change, there is a certain amount of unpredictability involved. In practical terms, SegWit activation will affect the price of Bitcoin one way or another in the short term, however at the time of writing, SegWit has only been activated for less than 72 hours, and the price has held stable thus far.

The activation of SegWit could well pave way for the lightning network, a technology that will enable instant Bitcoin transactions. Instant transactions as previously stated, will help micro and nano transactions immensely, and allow small businesses to utilize the benefits of accepting payments in Bitcoin at point of sale terminals. This will be especially useful in countries with low-value fiat currencies. One current example of this is Venezuela, where the Venezuelan Bolivar has lost around 90% of its value against the US dollar in under a year. Bitcoin transactions are helping a small, but significant portion of Venezuelan public hold value in the money they do have.

So what is Bitcoin Cash then?

Bitcoin Cash (BCH or BCC on exchanges) is a spin-off cryptocurrency that was the result of the August 1st hard fork by a small, yet significant proportion of the Bitcoin mining community. The fork involves increased block sizes and faster transaction times which in turn will lead to lower transaction fees. The blocksize has increased to 8MB, from the original 1MB that Bitcoin uses. This fork was designed to solve the scalability problems that Bitcoin currently faces.

So if Bitcoin Cash is technologically superior to Bitcoin, why don't I invest in that instead?

It's a tough question to answer because quite frankly, these are still very early days. At the time of writing the fork is only 1 month old and Bitcoin Cash has had high price fluctuations. Liquidity is much lower than Bitcoin (meaning it is difficult to sell large amounts) and real world adoption effects remain to be determined. If you're a new investor, Bitcoin Cash is certainly something to be monitored. However, the network effects of Bitcoin are still too strong to ignore, and it is still very much the number one cryptocurrency.

In terms of market price, the Bitcoin Cash split on August 1st initially led to a fall in the price of Bitcoin, before it once again rose to an all-time-high in late August. Bitcoin Cash value initially plummeted before a boom and then a reset to its current price of around $550.

If you purchased Bitcoin after August 1st, Bitcoin Cash should be treated as a completely separate currency. Any Bitcoin transaction will not be replicated in Bitcoin Cash or vice versa. If you wish to purchase Bitcoin, look for the symbol BTC on exchanges. If you purchased Bitcoin before August 1st you may well be able to receive the same amount in Bitcoin Cash - providing you held it in a wallet that was not linked to any exchange.

For miners, or those interested in mining, at the time of writing Bitcoin Cash offers greater mining rewards when compared to Bitcoin, due to a decreased difficulty in its proof-of-work algorithm.

How to Buy Bitcoin

Gone are the days when buying Bitcoin was a time consuming and somewhat uncomfortable endeavor. Nowadays buying Bitcoin is a similar process to exchanging currency when you go on vacation.

There are two ways to buy Bitcoin, the first is to use fiat currency (USD, EUR, GBP etc.) to purchase cryptocurrency via an exchange. These exchanges function the same way as regular foreign currency exchanges do. The prices fluctuate on a daily basis, and like regular currency exchange markets - they are open 24/7. These exchanges make their money from charging a small fee for each transaction.

Some charge both buyers and sellers, some only charge a fee for buying. For security reasons, most of these exchanges will require you to verify your ID before allowing you to purchase cryptocurrency.

It is also important to note the type of payments each exchange supports. Some allow for debit/credit card payments whereas other only accept PayPal or bank wire transfers. Below are the three biggest and reputable currency exchanges for purchasing Bitcoin,

Ethereum and other altcoins with fiat currency like US dollars, Euros or British Pounds.

Coinbase

Currently largest currency exchange in the world, Coinbase allows users to buy, sell and store cryptocurrency. Coinbase is undoubtedly the most beginner friendly exchange for anyone looking to get involved in the cryptocurrency market. They currently allow trading of Bitcoin, as well as, Ethereum and LiteCoin using fiat currency as a base. Known for their stellar security procedures and insurance policies regarding stored currency. The exchange also has a fully functioning iPhone and Android app for buying and selling on the go, very useful if you are looking to trade.

Once you are signed up and complete the identity verification procedures you can buy Bitcoin with your credit or debit card instantly.

If you sign up for Coinbase using this link, you will receive $10 worth of free Bitcoin after your first purchase of more than $100 worth of cryptocurrency.

http://bit.ly/10dollarbtc

Kraken

Based in Canada, and currently the largest exchange in terms of volume of buys in Euros, Kraken has the advantage of more coin support (they also allow the purchase of Monero, Ethereum Classic and Dogecoin) than Coinbase. It allows margin trading, which while beyond the scope of a beginner, will be of interest to more experienced traders

For other altcoins, you will need access to an exchange that facilitates cryptocurrency to cryptocurrency trading. The best one of these is Poloniex.

Poloniex

With more than 100 different cryptocurrencies available and data analysis for advanced traders, Poloniex is the most comprehensive exchange on the market. Low trading fees are another plus, this is a great place to trade your Bitcoin into other cryptocurrencies. If you have never purchased Bitcoin before, you will no be able to do so as Poloniex does not allow fiat currency deposits. Therefore, you will have to make your initial Bitcoin purchases on Coinbase or Kraken.

Buying Locally

The second way to buy Bitcoins in exchange for fiat currency is to locally purchase them in person. The advantage of this is that you may be able to get a marginally better price than by using an exchange. The other advantage is that users living in countries that don't have easy access to online exchanges can still buy coins in person. All transactions are protected by Escrow to prevent either party being scammed.

Website http://localbitcoins.com is the current market leader for local bitcoin transactions with sellers in over 15,000 cities around the world.

How To Safely Store Your Bitcoin

Congratulations on purchasing your first Bitcoins! Now that you've bought your Bitcoin, you'll need to keep it secure. You can do this by transferring it off the exchange and into what is known as a Bitcoin wallet. The name wallet implies that you can do all the same things you can with a regular wallet. You can see how much Bitcoin you have, and use it to spend your Bitcoin. An important distinction to make is that because Bitcoin is decentralized and stored on the Blockchain, these wallets do not "store" your Bitcoin per say.

While exchanges like Coinbase do provide you with your own wallet, unless you are day-trading, it's advisable to remove your coins from the exchange in order to prevent against issues like hacking - which unfortunately does happen

In 2011, Tokyo based Bitcoin exchange Mt. Gox suffered losses of over $27.2 million and 80,000 users lost a total of over $460 million worth of Bitcoin after the exchange was hacked. Mt. Gox wasn't some fly by night operation either, in fact at the time it was the largest cryptocurrency exchange on Earth. Yet poor security protocols and mismanagement allowed the attacks to occur. The company eventually filed for bankruptcy amid allegations of fraud, and much of the userbase's stolen coins have not been recovered to this day. This is why it's paramount that if you want to hold your coins for the long-term, you store them safely.

The understand wallets, we must first understand just how they work. Bitcoin transactions need both a private key (from the sender) and a public key (from the receiver) in order to process correctly on the blockchain.

A public key is a series of between 26 and 35 alphanumeric characters e.g. 1Co5CmEZNz35Am59EcFhKGRdNfLrzppGkJ

If you can this address to someone, they can send funds to your wallet. It is perfectly safe for you to give your public key, also known as your wallet address, to anyone, as they can only deposit into your account with this information. In 2013, a college student received 22 Bitcoins (then worth around $24,000) by holding up a sign with his public key in the form of a QR code on an edition of ESPN's College Gameday.

Your private key on the other hand should be held by you, and you alone. **Never give your private key to anyone.**

There are numerous types of wallets you can use, here is a breakdown of each one.

Desktop Wallets

A desktop wallet are a convenient medium between moving your Bitcoins off an exchange, while not having to carry around additional information like with a paper or hardware wallet. You can think of these like a Bitcoin bank account on your computer. Most desktop wallets will encrypt your private keys for you to add an extra layer of security. Here is a run-down of some of the more popular desktop Bitcoin wallets. All the wallets listed below are free, you should never pay for a desktop wallet.

Electrum - https://electrum.org

While it's design may not win any awards, Electrum does the job it's supposed to. The code is open source, which means there's a much lower possibility of the development team slipping in something malicious. Electrum allows you to store and spend your Bitcoins with relative ease. It has the advantage of storing your private keys offline, and to go online in "watching only" mode, so if your computer gets hacked during the process, hackers won't be able to spend any coins. It also has support for various hardware wallets.

Exodus - https://www.exodus.io/

Unlike Electrum, Exodus is not open source. However, Exodus does have the advantage of being capable of storing other coins like Ethereum, Litecoin and Dogecoin in addition to Bitcoin. The interface is also more user-friendly than Electrum.

It should be noted, that as desktop wallets require your computer to be connected to the internet, they can never be 100% secure.

CoPay - https://copay.io

CoPay operates on both desktop and mobile platforms, so it's great if you're looking to spend or receive Bitcoins on the go. It requires multiple signatures (ways of account verification) to spend coins, which is an added security feature. There's a multiple user option as well, which is useful for groups and families. The software's code being open source is always a plus.

Paper Wallets

Paper wallets are simply notes of your private key that are written down on paper. They will often feature QR codes so the sender can quickly scan them to send cryptocurrency.

Pros:

- Cheap
- Your private keys are not stored digitally, and are therefore not subject to cyber-attacks or hardware failures.

Cons:

- Loss of paper due to human error
- Paper is fragile and can degrade quickly in certain environments
- Not easy to spend cryptocurrency quickly if necessary - not useful for everyday transactions

You can use sites like bitaddress.org to create non-secure paper wallets online. These are known as non-secure as you have to be connected to the internet in order to use them. If the site is hacked, then hackers can access information regarding all private keys that have ever been created.

Step by Step Guide on How to Create a 100% Secure Paper Wallet

Required Material:

- **Offline download of bitaddress -** http://bit.ly/offlinebitaddress

- **Lili Live USB -** http://www.linuxliveusb.com/en/download

- **Ubuntu Operating System -** http://www.ubuntu.com/download/desktop

- **USB Flash Drive -** either a brand new or one you are willing to format the existing data from

- **A printer**

Installing Ubuntu on your flash drive

1. Download the above programs

2. Open LiLi and insert your USB flash drive into your computer

3. In Lili choose a source - select "ISO/IMG/Zip" option

4. In Lili Options - select "Format the key in FAT32"

5. Unzip the offline bitaddress file and copy it into your flash drive

Then disconnect your computer from the internet - this is so there is no way anyone can access your computer while you are creating a private key.

Booting Ubuntu from your flash drive

Reboot your computer, and press F12 before windows or OSX loads. Select USB HDD from the boot menu. Then run the Ubuntu operating system from your flash drive. After it has loaded, click on "Try Ubuntu"

Once Ubuntu has loaded, click on system settings then printers and add your printer. Print out 1 page to test it has connected.

Creating your wallet

6. Click on the Firefox icon on Ubuntu and open the private browsing window

7. Type in the following in the address bar: **file:///cdrom/bitaddress.org-master/**

8. Click on "BitAddress.org.html"

9. Move your cursor around until the timer reaches 0 (this is to ensure that you are a real person)

10. Choose Paper Wallet

11. Follow the steps to print out your paper wallet

12. Deposit BTC using the public address on the left hand side of the wallet (represented by a QR code)

Additional Recommendations

It is recommended you store your paper wallet in a sealed plastic bag to protect against water or damp conditions. Make multiple copies for extra security and if you are holding cryptocurrency for the long-term, store the paper inside a safe.

Hardware Wallets

Hardware wallets refer to physical storage items that contain your private key. The most common form of these are encrypted USB sticks. These are similar to ones you can make yourself, except someone else has already set up the security protocols for you. This is ideal for those who are non-tech savvy. Many of them also have built-in backup software in case you lose your keys.

These wallets use two factor authentication or 2FA to ensure that only the wallet owner can access the data. For example, one factor is the physical USB stick plugged into your computer, and the other would be a 4 digit pin code - much like how you use a debit card to withdraw money from an ATM.

Pros:

● Near impossible to hack - as of the time of writing, there have been ZERO instances of hacked hardware wallets

● Even if your computer is infected with a virus or malware, the wallet cannot be accessed due to 2FA

- The private key never leaves your device or transfers to a computer, so once again, malware or infected computers are not an issue

- Can be carried with you easily if you need to spend your cryptocurrency

- Transactions are easier than with paper wallets

- Can store multiple addresses on one device - good if you plan on having multiple Bitcoin accounts

- For the gadget lovers among you - they look a lot cooler than a folded piece of paper

Cons:

- More expensive than paper wallets - starting at around $60

- Susceptible to hardware damage, degradation and changes in technology

- Different wallets support different cryptocurrencies

- Trusting the provider to deliver an unused wallet. Using a second hand wallet is a big security breach. Only purchase hardware wallets from official sources.

The most popular of these are the Trezor and Ledger wallets. Both of these provide an easy to use experience in addition to being a portable and secure way to store your Bitcoin.

How to Trade Bitcoin

While you may want to hold Bitcoin for the long term, you may also wish to trade them for other cryptocurrencies or fiat currency. This is the fastest way to make money with Bitcoin, but also the riskiest. To trade for fiat currency, you can simply sell them at the current exchange rate on the same exchange you bought them at, like Coinbase or Kraken.

If you want to trade them for other cryptocurrencies however, it's best to move them to Poloniex or another large exchange like Bittrex. Once on here you will see the exchange rate between Bitcoin and other currencies. It should be noted that this may differ from the exchange rate for the cryptocurrency to fiat pairing. For example, the exchange rate for BTC to Litecoin (LTC) may differ from the rate for BTC/USD and LTC/USD. Fees are usually low for crypto-to-crypto trades, the maximum fee on Poloniex for example is 0.25%.

Another element you should examine is the liquidity for certain pairings. For example, you don't want a trade to be delayed because someone on the exchange is not selling the volume of the coin you are buying. To check liquidity of certain coin pairings go to http://coinmarketcap.com

These exchanges also along you to view the historical price charts for the various pairings as well as the liquidity (ease of making a trade) for each market.

As with any speculative market, trading Bitcoin is risky and you are liable to lose money. This is especially true if you trade on emotion, and not rationality. It is advisable to proceed with caution and do your homework before you do any trading for real. You can practice with virtual money (known as paper trading) on sites like https://www.whaleclub.co/

Needless to say though, you will make mistakes at first. You'll learn from these mistakes, but it's important that you make them with money you can afford to lose.

If you are going to trade, take intermediate profits for yourself. This way any gains you have made are in your bank account, and not just on paper. Dollar cost averaging also applies to trading in addition to investing.

What Determines the Price of Bitcoin?

If you're going to invest in Bitcoin, or any cryptocurrency for that matter, it's important to understand the market factors that drive the price one way or another. There are a number of these, which often interact with one another, but for simplicity purposes, we will examine them one by one.

China

No country has more of an effect on the price of Bitcoin than China. More fiat to Bitcoin trades from China than any other country, and some of the largest exchanges in the world are based there. Approximately 70% of the world's Bitcoin trades occur in the Chinese market.

Good news from China equals good news for the market in general. A December 2013 announcement from the People's Bank of China decreeing that Bitcoin was not a currency tanked the market by 35% in under an hour. Conversely, news of Bitcoin being adopted by Chinese business often leads to the Bitcoin price rising.

One major factor that makes China such a driving force in the Bitcoin market is the Chinese government's strict financial regulation of assets held in Chinese Yuan. Both wealthy and middle class Chinese citizens are looking for a way to secure their financial future without tying it to the value of the Yuan, which has been devalued in recent years. Bitcoin represents the perfect way for them to do this. Further Yuan devaluation will only lead to increased Bitcoin growth in the future.

Russia

Like China, Russia is also suffering from issues with its fiat currency, the ruble. The ruble has continued to fall against the US dollar year-on-year for the past 3 years. As it does so, Russians like to protect their wealth by moving their rubles into Bitcoin.

Adoption is Russia is also a major player in Bitcoin short-term price movements. An announcement in May 2017 that Ulmart, the largest online retailer in Russia, would begin accepting Bitcoin payments, took the market to a then all time high of $1800.

Government Regulation

Government support for Bitcoin will also play a part in the price of it as a commodity. Although Bitcoin is not tied to any one nation, for mass adoption to occur - it needs the support of government. The main contention for governments right now is Bitcoin's perceived "complete anonymity" and how it relates to crime, especially tax evasion. Once measures are in place to eliminate the anonymity element (regardless of your moral standpoint on this), government support will rise, and so will the price of Bitcoin.

Conversely, any time there is news of a government crackdown on Bitcoin either as a digital currency, or on a technology level - the price decreases

Technological Innovation

Advances in the Bitcoin network are vital if it is to continue increasing in value. As previously mentioned, new developments like SegWit and the lighting network, which will ease scalability issues, are important in the development of the coin on a technological front.

The coin's ability to handle micropayments (transactions of small monetary value) is one key area that was have a big effect on the future value. Currently the effectiveness of the system for micropayments is limited by the 1MB block size, which leads to minimum transaction amounts and delays in payment processing if you send too many transactions too quickly. With the implementation of lightning network, the team hopes to ease these issues and further increase Bitcoin's real world viability.

Mass Media

Despite what we'd like to believe, the vast majority of society still get their news from just 1 or 2 sources. To put it bluntly, the mainstream media doesn't understand Bitcoin one iota. Due to the lack of proper cryptocurrency or crypto asset journalists working for major outlets, they would rather give airtime to good soundbites like "Bitcoin could reach $100,000 within 5 years" or inversely "Bitcoin is the biggest bubble since the dotcom craze" than examine it at a technological level, or focus on any innovations that have been made. Positive news for Bitcoin in the media leads to new investors, and negative news leads to a decrease in price.

The other side of this is that some Bitcoin commentators have already made up their mind without even examining the technology. If you see an article in 2017 talking about Bitcoin as a front for "drug dealing" or "money laundering", then you can safely disregard it.

For your own personal news source, I recommend dedicated sites like http://coindesk.com for legitimate, non-biased or overhyped news regarding Bitcoin and cryptocurrency.

Funding for Blockchain Companies

As blockchain companies continue to receive more funding and investment, the currency receives more legitimization. Many blockchain related startups now accept investments in Bitcoin and other cryptocurrencies like Ethereum.

The Middle Class Investor

An often overlooked factor. While Bitcoin may be increasing in popularity among younger investors and some larger institutions, it is still very much off the radar of the American middle class. In other words think about Tom, aged 55, from Maryland. He's married and has a low 6 figure income from his upper management job. His portfolio currently consists mainly of blue chip stocks and low-cost index funds. He's not trying to hit any home runs, he's just trying to shore up his retirement assets. Once Bitcoin cements its reputation as a form of "digital gold" and more of a solid long-term investment rather than the speculative play thing it is seen as by some major institutions, it's value will continue to rise. In other words, we need more people like Tom as our target Bitcoin buyer for the value to continue increasing.

Technical Analysis

It should be noted that traditional technical analysis or chart analysis like one would do on stocks is tough, as the cryptocurrency market is a) only 8 years old so lacks comprehensive data and b) unlike anything we've ever seen before. However, charting does have its place in the Bitcoin universe and I would recommend you study stock technical analysis books if you are planning to trade Bitcoin on a serious level, with candlestick charting being the most useful for the cryptocurrency market.

Mass Adoption

As more merchants accept Bitcoin as a means of payment, the more it legitimizes the currency. Bitcoin's scalability issues will be the main determinant of this. Adoption shows no sign of slowing down and the total number of businesses accepting the currency continues to grow. If corporate giants such as Amazon and Apple began to accept Bitcoin payments, then the price is likely to increase once again.

Bitcoin for Business: How Your Business can Benefit from Accepting Bitcoin Payments

If you're not a small business owner, you can skip this section, but if you are, I advise you to pay close attention.

First and foremost, accepting Bitcoin payments can save you money.

While traditional credit card payment processing are around 2-3%. Using Bitcoin payment platforms such as BitPay can reduce these fees to around 1%. Even a small percentage change like this can represent big savings in the long run. If you're an internet seller tired of bank's charging you extortionate fees for currency conversions, or simply want to make your product or service accessible worldwide - Bitcoin may be your solution. Bitcoin doesn't discriminate across borders, and payments from any countries are subject to the same transaction costs.

There are millions of Bitcoin users looking for places to spend their coins, adding your business to the equation can only be good for the network as a whole. Bitcoin users are also an enthusiastic bunch, and enjoy supporting businesses that accept it. Cryptocurrency as a whole is a growing market, and making your business an early adopter is a chance to become a player in your industry via increased brand awareness.

There's also protection against chargeback fraud. As Bitcoin payments are irreversible, you, the merchant is no longer responsible for the costs of fraud.

For non-profits, Bitcoin donations have soared year-on-year since its inception. The Jamaican Bobsled team funded their trip to the 2014 Winter Olympics entirely from cryptocurrency donations. There's also the benefits of customers seeing the total donation amount and where it is spent in a sector where transparency is king.

If you're worried about the fluctuation of Bitcoin's value, then services like BitPay have you covered with daily bank transfers in your local currency.

Can I Still Make Money with Bitcoin in 2017?

Short answer: Yes

Long answer: Bitcoin continues to grow, both as a digital asset and as a currency with real world applications. Increased globalization and the need to transfer money across borders will only lead to a rise in adoption of Bitcoin. The amount of cross border money transfers continues to grow year-on-year and now represent almost 1% of the world's GDP. Bitcoin's total market cap now stands at $71 billion, more than the GDP of countries like Costa Rica and Bulgaria.

The near (but not total) anonymous element of Bitcoin is another factor that continues to drive growth. This is particularly important in countries where government's heavily regulate the fiat currency like China.

Bitcoin has now become a brand in and of itself. The currency is synonymous with a digital store of value. This is something that no other cryptocurrency can touch. Think of it like buying a property. Would you rather buy one in a "name brand" city like London or New York, where the demand for properties like yours will always be high, regardless of the general state of the market. Or one for the same price in say Oklahoma City where you may be able to buy a bigger house - but will you be able to sell during a market downturn?

Whether you want to use Bitcoin as a tool for trading, exchanging for other cryptocurrencies or as a long term store of value, there has never been a better time to invest in cryptocurrency than 2017. It's also never been easier to invest with sites like Coinbase and Kraken.

Just remember though, everyone feels like a genius or ahead of the curve when the market is going up. There will be down periods, and it's important to manage your risk correctly so that you can ride out the bad times and continue to profit during the good ones. Remember this - even the best in the business get it wrong sometimes

The Bitcoin Investing Mindset and How to Minimize Your Risk

In a market as volatile as cryptocurrency, it's important to minimize your risk as much as possible. With potential market changes of 10% on a daily basis, it's important for your portfolio, as well as, your peace of mind.

First off, never invest more than you can afford to lose. It may be tempting to try and hit a home run, but in doing so you will cause yourself sleepless nights and anxiety ridden days.

Secondly, unless you are day trading, don't check crypto price charts every few hours. Doing so will only give additional anxiety. The price is liable is swing by large percentage margins on a daily basis, that's just the way of the Bitcoin market, just remember that so far, over the long run, the price has continued to increase.

Dollar Cost Averaging

One of the best ways to minimize your risk in a volatile market is to use what is known as 'dollar cost averaging'. This simply means dividing up your total planned investment and buying Bitcoin at regular intervals instead of all at once.

With dollar cost averaging, you are simply buying less of an asset (in this case, Bitcoin) when the price is high, and more when the price is low. Your total exposure is less because you are only exposed to part of any decline in the market, as opposed to all of it with a lump sum investment. Your average cost per coin is therefore likely to be lower.

Let's use an example, both Alan and John have $1200 to invest in Bitcoin at the start of 2015. Alan decides to invest all $1200 on January 1st, John on the other hand is going to use dollar cost averaging. He will invest $100 on the 1st of each month, for a total of $1200. The prices used in this example are the actual Bitcoin trading prices as of those dates.

January 1st 2015 - $305.32

February 1st 2015 - $237.18

March 1st 2015 - $263.57

April 1st 2015 - $255.23

May 1st 2015 - $226.45

June 1st 2015 - $233.44

July 1st 2015 - $260.73

August 1st 2015 -$283.04

September 1st 2015 - $229.00

October 1st 2015 - $240.10

November 1st 2015 - $325.28

December 1st 2015 - $375.95

Alan's total investment in BTC = 3.93 (1200/305.32)

John's total investment in BTC = 4.55 (1200/269.60)

Price on January 1st 2016 - $433.57

Alan's Portfolio Value = 3.93*433.57 = $1704.02

John's Portfolio Value = 4.55*433.57 = $1974.37

Alan's ROI = 42%

John's ROI = 64.5%

So by using dollar cost averaging, John's average BTC purchase price was $269.60, whereas Alan bought a lump sum at $305.32. By having a lower average purchase price, John's ROI is higher over time. Alan bought her coins at the peak of the market before a prolonged downturn, whereas John utilized this downturn to his advantage.

Remember, time in the market beats timing the market. Generally speaking, the longer you are invested in something, the better.

FOMO & FUD

These are two terms you should become familiar with if you are going to be investing and trading in Bitcoin, or any cryptocurrency for that matter.

FOMO - Fear Of Missing Out

This is most commonly manifested when you see news reports of <insert hot shiny new altcoin here> increasing by ridiculous numbers like 100+% in a day. It may be tempting to trade a proportion or even all (terrible idea) your Bitcoin in for the latest cool cryptocurrency object, but it's incredibly risky. Many smaller altcoins are backed up by purely theoretical technology, and have no real world adoption for whatever product or service they are backing. Remember to do your due diligence regarding coin news. Just because the headline might read "Amazing Altcoin linked to Amazon deal", doesn't necessarily mean the deal is anywhere close, or if there even is a deal in the first place. Check your facts before investing.

It is important to understand that Bitcoin has now reached a point where there are real world uses, and it is by far the most adopted out of any cryptocurrency. Therefore, Bitcoin has greater market saturation and thus is unlikely to skyrocket in value like smaller coins. The opposite is also true though and with great rewards comes great risk. Many smaller coins can, and do lose up to 80% of their value in just a few days (for further reading check out the Chaincoin pump and dump scheme of July 2017), whereas Bitcoin continues to hold strong. If you are planning to buy and hold a single coin for the long term, Bitcoin should be your only play.

FUD - Fear, Uncertainty & Doubt

FUD is the spreading of misinformation by uninformed sources. Many of these sources have their own nefarious reasons for doing so. It may be to promote an alternative coin, or they may have shorted (bet on the price decreasing) Bitcoin. Of course, legitimate criticism of Bitcoin as a technology is fine, and should be encouraged if the technology is to advance. FUD however is mostly slander and baseless accusations about Bitcoin as a technology, the people behind it or the people invested in it.

How can you avoid FUD? Simply by obtaining your Bitcoin and other cryptocurrency news from reliable sources, who don't have a vested interest one way or another. It is important to use multiple sources to get a well rounded view of the situation.

Investing your Bitcoin - ICOs

An ICO or Initial Coin Offering, is an alternative form of crowdfunding that many blockchain startups have been utilizing as of late. Instead of donating in US Dollars in return for shares of the company, patrons can donate in Bitcoin or other cryptocurrencies in exchange for new tokens of the company.

The most famous ICO thus far was the Ethereum ICO of July 2014. Ethereum is a new blockchain based platform that allows applications and automatically executed contracts, known as "smart contracts" to be built on it. During the funding phase, Ethereum received roughly 31,500 Bitcoin, equivalent to $18.4 million at the time. In return, a total of 60 million Ethereum tokens were distributed to those who were part of the funding. The project has been extremely successful in the short term and today, 60 million Ethereum is worth approximately $24 billion.

ICOs represent a way for companies to fund their blockchain projects, in addition to providing returns for investors. Usually the offerings last for a period of a few weeks, and the company issuing the new tokens will have a goal amount that they aim to raise. ICOs have rapidly increased in popularity in the past 18 months, and 2017 is on track to be the first year that blockchain companies raise more money from ICOs than they do from traditional venture capitalists. For an investment purpose, ICOs represent a way for savvy investors to get in on the ground floor of an exciting new project.

The downside of this of course, is that with so many new ICOs popping up, some of them have far less legitimacy than others. If you are planning to invest in an ICO, do so based on the underlining usefulness of the project, and not any fancy marketing buzzwords that the company uses in their sales copy. Just because something is based on a blockchain platform, does not always mean there is a real world demand for the product or service. Another area to examine is the team of developers behind the project, and their track record of successfully developing blockchain applications.

Like any traditional startup venture, more ICOs will fail than succeed, and raising money is only part of a successful project. One such example of an ICO with problems is Bancor, an ICO based of the idea of creating a market-making (generating an automatic buy and sell price) product that provided liquidity for digital assets. The project raised a staggering $153m in just 3 hours, over 50% higher than the initial target.

However the project had problems with investor's transactions being accepted in addition to the Bancor team issuing extra token after the funding period was complete. This ultimately means a lower returns for investors. Like any investment, is important to do your due diligence before becoming involved, and never invest more than you can afford to lose. One final word, like anything in the Bitcoin or cryptocurrency space, ICOs are not a get rich quick scheme.

Lately the ICO buzz has been so intense that there are even ICOs utilizing Facebook Ads and celebrity endorsements in an attempt to gain investment. It's worth asking yourself if you would invest in a non-blockchain company based on a Facebook advertisement, and I think you already know the answer. If a company's main selling point is "amazing returns", rather than technological innovation, then it's likely to be a sub-par investment rather than a solid one.

The other area that is vital to understand, is that you ARE NOT buying stock in these companies during the ICO phase. You don't own any of the company, you simply own whatever token they denominize which will fluctuate in value due to external factors that go behind the company's own performance.

Why I Don't Recommend You Mine Bitcoin

Whenever Bitcoin's price is rising (and that's most of the time!), the mining question always pops up. Usually from those who are inexperienced or want a "free" way to get a piece of the pie.

It all starts with a variant of this question

"Why buy Bitcoin at $100/$1,000/$4,000 when you can just use your computer to mine some for free?"

Unfortunately, like everything else - there is no such thing as free Bitcoin.

As previously discussed, the way Bitcoins are created or "mined" is by using a computer to solve an of increasingly complex series of algorithms. Users are then rewarded for solving these algorithms by receiving Bitcoin. There is no man power involved, you yourself don't have to solve the algorithm, you just have to link your computer up to the Bitcoin network and the computer does the rest. There are also no shortcuts or breakthrough moments, the only way Bitcoin can be obtained quicker is with more computer power. How much computational power you supply determines the size of your reward. The more power you supply, the more Bitcoins you receive.

Now here is why mining is generally a terrible investment for the average Joe.

1. Electricity Costs - The electricity costs involved with running your computer 24/7 (which is necessary for mining) by far outweigh the amount of Bitcoins you receive for completing the task. You require access to industrial electricity rates of around $0.02 per kWh in order for the venture to be profitable on a small scale.

2. Requiring Specialist Hardware - Nowadays, the most efficient mining processes require special hardware known as Application-specific integrated circuits (ASIC). ASICs can be described as a supercomputer that can only ever perform one task. Specialist Bitcoin ASIC miners available for consumer purchase still start at around $1000 and often run around $2000-$2500.

3. Equipment maintenance - To maintain all this computing power is an additional cost. The cost of cooling alone is a large cost that has to be factored in to long term profits. Hardware running 24/7 burns out faster and replacement mining equipment will be needed in due course.

4. The increasing size of the Bitcoin network - The network pays out a fixed amount of Bitcoin, regardless of how many miners are using the network. The current rate is around 1800BTC per day, which sounds like a huge number, until you realise just how many miners there are on the network. The current mining power is equivalent to 17.6 BILLION desktop computers. Therefore the average payout for the end user running 1 desktop computer full time is around approximately $0.000107 per day. Or roughly 2 cents a year's worth of BTC. To put it lightly, you have more chance of winning the lottery than you do making a profit from mining Bitcoin your standard home computer.

Mining in 2017 is a much different proposition from mining in 2010 or even 2012. There are some opportunities which involved investing in Bitcoin farms or group purchasing processing power of ASIC at a discount. This is known as a "mining pool". Due to cheaper power costs, currently around 80% of the world's mining pools are based in China, with Iceland possessing the second largest number. Joining a mining pool requires a lower upfront investment but still requires cheap electricity rates and have debatable ROI potential.

It should also be worth noting that many of those who promote group mining or cloud mining do so under an affiliate program with whatever company that are promoting, meaning they get a commission % every time someone signs up.

However, for the average Joe without a huge amount of money to invest - I would strongly recommend buying coins instead of mining them. You are more likely to get higher returns in both the short and long run.

Is there a Bitcoin ETF or Mutual Fund I can invest in?

Exchange Traded Funds (ETFs) and mutual funds have represented some of the safest investments over the past few decades. Instead of investing in individual companies, you are buying an aggregate share of many companies. By allowing for this level of diversification, this represents a low risk use of your funds, and for many years investors have been clamoring for a Bitcoin or cryptocurrency fund like this due to the price volatility of individual cryptocurrencies.

Unfortunately attempts for a Bitcoin ETF have been thwarted by regulatory bodies thus far. In 2017, two Bitcoin ETF applications were rejected by the SEC. The reasoning from the government body was the lack of regulation and market surveillance in the cryptocurrency space.

The closest thing to a Bitcoin mutual fund today is a diversified fund offered by http://thetoken.io based out of Russia - the fund is a combination of 16 different cryptocurrency tokens, with Ethereum (22%) and Bitcoin (17%) representing the largest portions of the fund. Investments can be made with both BTC and ETH and funds are stored in Ethereum backed wallets. However, fiat currency investments are not currently supported. The fund is backed by a smart contract on the Ethereum platform to ensure the legitimacy of the tokens offered.

However, the main drawback of the site is that it is not available to those based in the US or Singapore, although this may change in the future based on the regulatory status of Bitcoin and other cryptocurrencies. Once again, like any investments you are liable to lose money in a market downturn, so only invest money you are comfortable losing.

The Ten Commandments of Bitcoin

If you get nothing else from this book, at least follow these rules and you'll be in a better position to make money than other new investors.

1. **Thou shalt believe in Bitcoin at a technological level**

2. **Thou shalt never gives one's private key to anyone else**

3. **Thou shalt always stay informed with Bitcoin news from reputable sources**

4. **Thou shalt never panic sell during a downturn**

5. **Thou shalt always take intermediate profits for oneself**

6. **Thou shalt always store cryptocurrency safely**

7. **Thou shalt not spend every hour checking cryptocurrency markets**

8. Thou shalt never mine Bitcoin on their regular desktop computer

9. Thou shalt not invest more than you can afford to lose

10. Thou shalt always help others with less knowledge than yourself

Conclusion

Bitcoin has changed the way we look at money and finance. Our previous reliance on banks and other financial institutions has been put into question. These long standing financial institutions now face unprecedented disruption from this groundbreaking technology. For users, cross border payments at a near-instant transaction time and far lower transactions fees are making the global economy smaller. For merchants, protecting themselves from fraud has never been easier with the rise of Bitcoin. Even non-profits can benefit hugely from Bitcoin as a payment method. Blockchain technology has an additional laundry list of benefits ranging from transparency in elections to easily accessible medical records between parties.

As a commodity, Bitcoin has produced unrivaled returns for investors over the past 7 years. No other financial asset, in the cryptocurrency space or otherwise has made more people money since its inception in 2010. For those who believe in Bitcoin, long may these returns continue.

I hope you've enjoyed this book and that you're now a little bit more informed about how Bitcoin works, and more importantly, how it can work for you.

Whether you're planning on investing for the long-term, or hoping to make short-term gains by trading - I wish you the best of luck.

Remember, trade rationally and not emotionally. Never invest more than you can afford to lose, and for the love of God - don't check the charts 15 times a day.

If you're ready to make the next step and get involved in the market. I have a small gift for you.

If you sign up for Coinbase using this link, you will receive $10 worth of free Bitcoin after your first purchase of more than $100 worth of cryptocurrency.

http://bit.ly/10dollarbtc